THE FIRST WORLD WAR AT SEA
IN PHOTOGRAPHS

1916

THE FIRST WORLD WAR AT SEA IN PHOTOGRAPHS

1916

PHIL CARRADICE

AMBERLEY

First published 2014

Amberley Publishing
The Hill, Stroud
Gloucestershire, GL5 4EP

www.amberley-books.com

British Library Cataloguing in Publication Data.
A catalogue record for this book is available from the British Library.

ISBN 978 1 4456 2242 2 (print)
ISBN 978 1 4456 2265 1 (ebook)

Typesetting and Origination by Amberley Publishing.
Printed in Great Britain.

Contents

Introduction

The year 1916 began with a tacit acknowledgement that, as far as Britain was concerned, voluntary enlistment – mainly in the Army but to an extent in the Navy as well – was never going to be enough to win the war. Hopes of a victory by Christmas had dissolved amid the cynical comment, 'Which Christmas?'

The bill to sanction conscription was passed through Parliament on 6 January, along with several resignations as some ministers regarded formal conscription as a clear intrusion on the liberty of the individual. The original legislation had been intended to cover just single men over the age of eighteen but by May the age limit had been increased and extended to married men as well.

The restriction of individual liberty was something of a hot topic in the first few months of the year. The U-boat blockade was beginning to impinge on the supply of foodstuffs and already there were shortages. It was not much different in Germany, however, as the blockade by the Royal Navy was both effective and remorseless. There were rumours of food riots in Berlin and other large cities, and food rationing had been introduced into Germany at the end of 1915.

The final evacuation from the Gallipoli Peninsula took place on 8 January, soldiers and sailors alike being more than happy to leave the godforsaken wilderness to which, for the past nine months, they had been condemned. British naval campaigns in the area continued, however, submarine patrols into the Sea of Marmara being particularly effective.

The German submarine campaign was also stepped up in the early months of 1916. On 21 February the USA was informed that, in future, any defensively armed merchant ships would be regarded as cruisers and therefore were liable to immediate attack from hidden U-boats. On 1 March the German extended submarine campaign began, an action that was ultimately more responsible than anything else for bringing America into the war.

One of the least celebrated heroes of the war was Admiral Reginald Hall, the man in charge of naval intelligence. From Room 40 at the Admiralty, Hall and his team of codebreakers maintained a close watch on German fleet movements and passed on vital information to Jellicoe and the men in charge of the battle fleets. It was Hall who informed the Grand Fleet that the Germans were on the move at the end of May.

As a consequence, by far the most significant event in the naval war took place on 31 May, when the British and German fleets at last came into contact at the Battle of Jutland. This monumental clash of the titans had been inevitable – and looked forward to, eagerly, by men on both sides – but, perhaps not surprisingly, the battle ended in an indecisive stalemate. The two fleets were far too valuable to risk outright destruction.

The Germans took the initiative when Admiral Reinhard Scheer decided to send his battlecruisers – the Scouting Force, as it was known – into the Skagerrak between Denmark and Norway. Vice Admiral Franz von Hipper's job was to pull the British battlecruisers into a general chase, which would end when they came under the guns of Scheer's High Seas Fleet. It was an ingenious plan as Admiral David Beatty, in charge of the British battlecruiser fleet, was not the man to refuse such a challenge.

Battle was joined at 3.48 on the afternoon of 31 May when the two battlecruiser squadrons came within sight of each other off the Skagerrak. Beatty, on board the *Lion*, had six battlecruisers and, a little further astern, the four fast battleships of the 5th Battle Squadron. Hipper, commanding from the *Seydlitz*, had only five battlecruisers but his intention was not to stand and fight. He and Scheer had bigger games to play.

The opening salvoes were fired at a range of over 8 miles and, although seeming to be running for their lives, the German shooting was surprisingly accurate. The *Lion* and *Tiger* were severely damaged and within the space of half an hour both the *Indefatigable* and the *Queen Mary* took hits, exploded and sank.

Beatty's now-famous remark to his Flag Captain, Chatfield – 'There seems to be something wrong with our bloody ships today' – has gone down in history. There were just eleven survivors from the two ships. As if that was not bad enough, another of Beatty's battlecruisers, the *Invincible*, was also later hit and lost.

It was not all one-way traffic. The *Seydlitz*, *Derfflinger* and *Lützow* were all severely damaged and set on fire. The damage to the *Lützow* was so severe that, with no hope of making it back to Wilhelmshaven, she was sunk by her own forces. The battleship *Pommern* was also sunk, torpedoed by British destroyers.

When it was almost too late, Beatty realised he was being led into a trap and reversed course, now leading the German High Seas Fleet under the guns of Jellicoe and his battleships. At 18.27, as light began to fail, the two giant fleets finally came into contact with each other. Scheer saw his danger, however, and immediately crossed to the stern of the British fleet and escaped.

Jellicoe did not pursue his enemy with any great conviction. He knew how valuable the fleet was to Britain, and the threat of U-boats in the vicinity was enough to keep him from a full-scale chase. Although the action continued throughout the night, most of the damaged German 'big ships' managed to limp away so that when dawn broke on 1 June Jellicoe was left in command of the sea.

The British lost three battlecruisers, three armoured cruisers and eight destroyers in the battle. A total of 6,097 men had been killed. The Germans' casualty list was one battlecruiser, one battleship, four cruisers and five destroyers, 2,545 of their sailors losing their lives. Clearly, in terms of ships and men lost, it was a German victory. However, their ships had suffered far more damage and Scheer never ventured out of port again. Strategically, then, Jutland was a clear victory for the British.

In the wake of the battle there was an immediate enquiry to find out why three British battlecruisers had exploded with such a catastrophic loss of life. This was conducted by the Third Sea Lord, Frederick Tudor, and other senior officers.

Various theories have been propounded over the years, ranging from the inadequate armour on the British battlecruisers to the high volatility of their propellant, from the removal of anti-flash doors to splinters from a number of direct hits on the thinly armoured turrets of the ships igniting the ammunition supply.

There might be an element of truth in all of these suggestions but it now seems as if the British obsession with rapid fire – invariably at the expense of accuracy – led not only to cordite being removed from its protective casings before action began but also to unprotected charges being stacked on deck and inside gun turrets. In addition, in order to hasten the delivery of shells to the guns, the doors to the magazines were always left open. In effect, the battlecruisers were little more than bombs, waiting to go off.

There is no doubt that Beatty (along with other senior officers) was keen for his ships to shoot as quickly as possible at Jutland. The battlecruisers might be the fastest firing ships in the Navy but their accuracy was abysmal and only a few weeks before Jutland the captain of the *Tiger* had been reprimanded after bad returns in gunnery practice. So, in a fleet engagement like Jutland, the risk of 'flash fires' was simply ignored.

Admiral Tudor's report was not welcomed by the Royal Navy. In effect, he was saying that the sailors – and the officers, senior and junior, who agreed to what were highly dangerous practices – had contrived their own destruction.

Far better, thought Jellicoe – who had risen to the post of First Sea Lord soon after the battle – to blame the construction of the ships, thereby apportioning blame to no single individual. The report was suppressed and Tudor was even forced to write a letter of apology to Beatty for any implied criticism. Soon afterwards, he was posted to the backwater of the China Fleet. The myth about poor deck armour on the battlecruisers simply grew and grew.

Germany claimed the victory at Jutland but, as the months went on and the High Seas Fleet did not emerge again, it became clear to everyone that the victory – if victory it was – remained a pyrrhic one. Scheer and Hipper knew that they had been lucky, lucky that Beatty's inept tactics had played into their hands and lucky that Scheer had been able to escape from the clutches of the more cautious Jellicoe. Not for nothing did Churchill later write that Jellicoe was the only man who could have lost the war in a single afternoon. Scheer and Hipper knew that they could not risk another encounter with the Grand Fleet.

From Jutland onwards, the German effort at defeating Britain rested in the hands of her submariners. The U-boat campaign increased in ferocity so that by the end of the year an average of 190,000 tons of British or Allied shipping was being sunk every month.

When the cruiser *Hampshire* was mined off the Orkneys in June she took with her to the bottom Field Marshal Kitchener, the British Minister for War. The mine had been laid by a German submarine with the express intention of catching the Grand Fleet as it left base. The mine got the *Hampshire* instead.

Mines laid by submarines were an example of how warfare was changing. Kitchener's death was, in itself, symbolic. He had been useful in the early days, his face adorning hundreds of recruiting posters. But by 1916 he was out of date and had been sidelined by other, more ambitious and more ruthless politicians like David Lloyd George. His day had gone.

January

On 6 January the pre-Dreadnought battleship *King Edward VII* was sunk when she hit a mine 25 miles off Cape Wrath. There was no loss of life, either in the explosion or in the subsequent abandoning of the ship before she sank. All the crew were taken off by escorting destroyers.

French soldiers are shown here leaving Gallipoli – the delight on their faces is obvious. For the moment, at least, they have escaped death. Unfortunately, the horrors of the Western Front and battles such as Verdun now await them.

Opposite above: Launched in 1905, the *King Edward VII* was unusual in that she was named after a reigning monarch. The king had been happy to lend his name to the ship, provided she would always be the flagship of any squadron in which she served. By 1916 she and her sister ships – the 'Wobbly Eight', as they were known, due to the whole class being poor sea boats – made up the 3rd Battle Squadron but were withdrawn from the Fleet before Jutland and stationed in the Thames to protect the coast from German battlecruiser raids.

Opposite below: By 8 January the evacuation of Allied troops from the Gallipoli Peninsula, which had begun the previous year, was complete. The Gallipoli campaign had been costly and ineffective from the start, thanks in the main to poor handling of troops and mismanagement of the whole affair by the men in charge. But it was not until an appalled and horrified Field Marshal Kitchener visited the peninsula in the autumn of 1915 that the decision to abandon the beachheads was made. The photograph shows Kitchener with General Birdwood at Anzac Cove during his visit.

The Gallipoli evacuation – British and Anzac troops collecting silently on the beaches to await transport, with timing devices set on rifles and grenades back in the trenches to convince the Turks that the occupation was continuing – was the most effective part of the whole campaign. The tragedy of Gallipoli was that nobody had used the same initiative to make the campaign a success.

A composite set of photographs showing Turkish troops in the wake of the Gallipoli evacuation. The successful defence of Gallipoli and the Dardanelles turned the Turkish commander, Mustafa Kemal Atatürk, into a national figure. In the years after the war, with the last sultan deposed and the war hero installed as the first president of the new Turkish Republic, he was the man who brought Turkey, screaming and kicking, into the twentieth century.

The abandoning of the Gallipoli campaign was greeted with relief and rejoicing from Allied and Turkish soldiers alike. This postcard view shows a thanksgiving service on the deck of one of the British battleships off Gallipoli, prior to making its way back across the Mediterranean.

February

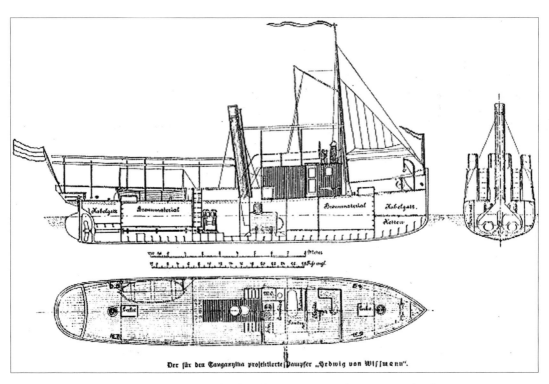

Der für den Tanganyika projektierte Dampfer „Hedwig von Wissmann".

A little-known naval campaign took place between December 1915 and February 1916 on and around Lake Tanganyika in central Africa. It was a war fought mainly by gunboats and motorboats from the forces of Britain and Belgium on the one side and Germany on the other. The largest and most powerful of these ships was the German *Hedwig von Wissman*. The architect's plans for the gunboat are shown here.

The lake had been dominated by German forces since the outbreak of war but, under the leadership of the eccentric Commander Geoffrey Spicer Simson, things were soon to change. Simson, who often wore a khaki kilt, flew an admiral's flag outside his tent and acquired a whole range of outlandish tattoos during his time in Africa, was nothing if not an energetic leader, and knew that the German gunboats would have to be defeated in battle.

Opposite: At Simson's request, two motorboats were ferried to South Africa and then sent northwards through the African bush to reach Lake Tanganyika. Transportation was by train, by paddling the boats up rivers and, when necessary, by manhandling through dense and dangerous terrain. The motorboats were called the *Mimi* and *Touton*, even though Simson had wanted to call them *Cat* and *Dog*. They are shown here being pulled through the jungle scrub.

There were two main engagements for 'Simson's Circus', as the small squadron was known, once the audacious commander got his gunboats to the lake. Firstly, the German *Kingani* was captured and taken to the British base where, rechristened HMS *Fifi*, she became an important part of the tiny British fleet.

On 9 February, the *Hedwig von Wissman* was ambushed as she cruised along the lake, and was overwhelmed by the *Mimi* and *Touton*. The above photograph shows the wrecked German vessel. Germany's other boat on the lake was scuttled following a bombing attack by Belgian aircraft. Soon afterwards the German forces were withdrawn and control over Lake Tanganyika passed to the Allies.

On 16 February, the War Office took over control of anti-aircraft defences for Britain. Previously this had rested in the hands of the Admiralty and while the change in emphasis did not prevent RNAS flyers from attempting to shoot down the Zeppelin raiders, it certainly relieved the Admiralty of an onerous and unwelcome responsibility.

On 21 February Germany informed the USA that in future any defensively armed merchant vessels, regardless of their nationality, would be regarded as 'cruisers' and would, therefore, be open to attack by U-boats. The announcement caused great anger in America – and great fear in the hearts of American capitalists, who could see their profits evaporating!

On 26 February the Royal Navy finished the evacuation of Serbian troops who had made a forced march to the Adriatic over the Albanian mountains through the coldest winter in living memory. This followed their defeat by German, Austro-Hungarian and Bulgarian forces. In an effort to reduce German influence in the region and to assist the Serbs in their fight, a combined Franco-British landing had already been made in Salonika.

Καλοκαιρινὰ Γαλλικὰ Νοσοκομεία   Hôpitaux Français d' été

Ελλὰς—Grèce   Souvenir Salonique

The Allied force arrived too late; the Serbs had already been beaten, and so once ashore in Salonika the French and British had nowhere to go. Faced by a powerful and determined Bulgarian army, they simply wired themselves in and allowed the Navy to supply them at regular intervals. The Kaiser, knowing they were troops that could be better employed elsewhere, called Salonika 'the largest internment camp in Europe'.

A ship-to-ship action took place on 29 February, 70 miles north-west of the Shetlands, when the German raider *Greif* and the British Armed Merchant Cruiser *Alcantara* went head to head in a bloody battle that saw no holds barred. Admiral Jellicoe had heard that the *Greif* had slipped out of port, past patrolling guard ships, and sent four vessels to intercept her. She was spotted by the *Alcantara*, the German ship being disguised as a Norwegian vessel, a deception that caused the British AMC to come too close and drop a boat crew over the side to investigate.

Before the British sailors arrived on board, the *Greif* suddenly opened fire, destroying the boat and its crew and causing serious damage to the *Alcantara*. The British ship was then hit by a torpedo and quickly sank. She had scored several hits on the *Greif*, however, disabling her and allowing the approaching *Andes* to close in and finally sink the raider. This shows the *Alcantara* in her pre-war role as a merchant ship, long before she encountered the *Greif*.

The battleship *Ramilles* is shown here with members of her crew standing on one of the gun turrets, the Forth Bridge in the background.

March

On 1 March, St David's Day, the extended German U-boat campaign began. From now on the German submarine attacks would be relentless. By the end of 1916, the sinking of vessels bound for Britain with vital cargoes was averaging 190,000 tons per month. This shows one of the deadly enemy submarines, the U14, on the surface with her crew on deck for a spot of fresh air.

A painting by artist Willy Stower shows a German U-boat in the process of sinking an Allied troop transport in the Mediterranean.

Bruce Bairnsfather's humorous view of the submarine crisis – a classic example of the British soldier's ability to laugh in the face of adversity – shows two old sweats up to their waists in water. One of the men in the trench sagely remarks, 'They'll be torpedoing us if we stick 'ere much longer, Bill.'

They might have been denigrated and derided in Britain, but U-boats and their crews were regarded as heroes in Germany, as this view of a rowing boat in a pleasure park in Berlin clearly shows. The boat, like all of the others, has been named after one of the famous U-boats – in this case U9.

War or no war, the Navy carried on its time-honoured rituals, and honouring the dead was an important part of service life. This postcard shows a funeral parade of naval personnel.

April

Gas had first been used as an offensive weapon on the Western Front at the Second Battle of Ypres in 1915. It was never used at sea but precautions had to be taken. This shows sailors wearing masks on the deck of their ship.

On 1 April 1916 the Zeppelin L15 became the first airship to be brought down by gunfire when returning from a raid on London. She crash-landed in the Thames estuary, where her crew quickly surrendered to the *Olivine*, before being sunk and destroyed later in the day. By the spring of 1916 the myth of the invincible airships was already being broken, although the giant craft still had the power to terrify the British population.

The Gallipoli campaign might have been over but action against the Turks continued. On 14 April two RNAS aircraft carried out a bombing raid on Constantinople (Istanbul). Limited damage was inflicted but there was mass panic, as this drawing of the incident, first published in the *Tribuna Illustrata*, clearly shows.

The battlecruiser *Invincible* is shown here leaving the Tyne.

On 22 April the battlecruisers *Australia* and *New Zealand* were involved in a collision. As a result, the *Australia* had to be dry-docked and consequently missed the forthcoming Battle of Jutland.

„Seydlitz" nach der Skagerak-Schlacht
in der Wilhelmshavener Schleuse am 3. 6. 16.

Nachbildung verboten.
F. Finke W'haven. Roonstr. 16.

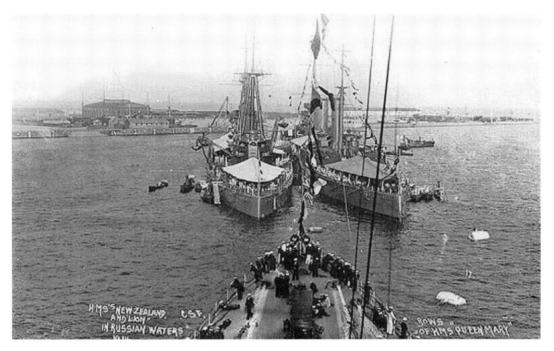

The *New Zealand*, paid for and presented by New Zealand, was not badly damaged in the collision with the *Australia*. She had already fought at the battles of Heligoland Bight and Dogger Bank and went on the serve at Jutland. This shows her alongside the *Lion*, the photograph having been taken from the battlecruiser *Queen Mary*.

Opposite above: Despite the British blockade, on 25 April Admiral Hipper in the *Seydlitz* – shown here in Wilhelmshaven – managed to lead a daring raid on the English coast. The coastal towns of Lowestoft and Yarmouth were bombarded and Hipper escaped back across the North Sea before scouting British forces could catch him.

Opposite below: Sir Roger Casement, philanthropist, explorer and former diplomat for the British Empire, became a fanatical Irish nationalist and in 1916 went to Germany to secure guns to help in an armed uprising against British rule. A total of 20,000 rifles were duly loaded on to the tiny *Aud*, along with several million rounds of ammunition. The *Aud* was intercepted by the sloop *Bluebell* before she could reach Ireland and the weapons lost when she was scuttled. Casement was captured and hung as a traitor. The planned rebellion went ahead without the German rifles.

Damage to houses can be clearly seen in this photograph taken after the German battlecruiser raids of 25 April.

Ships of the German High Seas Fleet are seen here in line of battle.

The damage to the centre of Dublin is seen here in the aftermath of the rising and the subsequent bombardment by British forces. Sackville Street is now O'Connell Street, Dublin's main shopping area.

During the Easter Rising, on 26 April the armed patrol vessel *Helga*, along with several batteries of RA guns, was called in to bombard the rebels holed up in the General Post Office and other strategic locations in Dublin. This shows the vessel at sea. Amazingly, the *Helga*, in a moment of supreme irony, was sold to the Irish Government in 1922.

The battleship *Russell*, along with the sloop *Nasturtium*, was sunk on 27 April off the coast of Malta. Once again it was mines that caused the problem, silent killers against which large capital ships seemed to have little or no defence.

The UC5 was a German minelaying submarine launched in June 1915 and which accounted for twenty-nine Allied warships (36,288 tons) with her mines in a period of about nine months. On 27 April 1916 she ran aground in the Channel and although her crew attempted to scuttle the vessel, she was captured by HMS *Firedrake* and brought into London, where she was displayed for the public at Temple Pier.

The UC5 was later taken to America, where she was put on display in New York. This shows the submarine, open to the public, in Central Park.

Dismantled for the trip across the Atlantic, the UC5 is shown here being rebuilt in Central Park, New York. Thousands of fascinated Americans came to walk around the submarine.

May

OUT FOR VICTORY.

THE MERCHANT SEAMAN.
Going home to sign on again.

Despite recent advances in coal and oil propulsion, in 1916 huge numbers of sailing ships still ploughed their way around the world's oceans. And many of the ships lost to German U-boats came from these sailing fleets. They were vessels which had little or no chance of escape once the submarines rose to the surface.

Opposite: The anger of merchant seamen at the callous German U-boat campaign is shown here in this postcard from the war years. Many sailors died while waiting for rescue, huddled in open boats and prey to all the elements. To make matters worse, the sailors' wages – regardless of whether they lived or died – were stopped by the shipping companies the moment their vessel went down.

Off Schleswig: British destroyers and seaplanes in action during a storm, March 25th, 1916.

The blockade of the German coast went on all year round, sailors enduring snow, wind and ice in the cruel waters of the North Sea.

Bomb damage to a British city after a Zeppelin raid.

THE RAIDER

PUBLICATION SANCTIONED BY OFFICIAL PRESS BUREAU.

PUBLISHING OFFICE: (Copyright)
39, ST. ANDREW'S HILL, E.C.

The battle against the Zeppelins was a relentless one, all manner of weapons, from aircraft to ships' guns, being used to shoot them down. Searchlights were an important part of the defence system and one Zeppelin is seen here, caught in the beam of those searchlights. On 4 May Zeppelin L7 was brought down by the guns of the cruisers *Galatea* and *Phaeton*. There were just seven survivors from the Zeppelin.

Scrubbing the decks – cleanliness was next to godliness in the Royal Navy and war or no war, decks had to be cleaned.

Opposite above: One of the least celebrated but most necessary duties of the Navy was transporting and escorting soldiers home from the Front for vital periods of rest and recuperation. This shows officers gathering at the leave train on Victoria station ready to begin the trip back to Dover, and then France.

Opposite below: Both sides used mines, thousands of these deadly weapons being dropped into the North Sea, the Channel and the Western Approaches. All manner of vessels, from submarines to destroyers, were used to lay the mines.

Series 2.

Britain's Might.

OUR Ships are the best that money can buy,
  And manned by stalwart crews;
We hold the **Keyes** of every sea,
  And are **Moore** than **Goodenough** 'tis true.

We are fighting a cause which is **Christain** and right,
  Against a foe who has shewn their breed,
By firing on hospitals and defenceless towns,
  And renowned by their brutality.

If they only will fight on sea with our might,
  We can **Beatty** the lot that is certain,
And their flouted pomp will like **Jelli-coe,**
  Which will make them ring down the curtain.

A British postcard using the names of well-known admirals to help make the poem that is in the centre of the card. The poem and the sentiments might be a little twee now but in 1916 cards like this were something that were eagerly collected by the public. Everyone would have known the names of the men mentioned.

Opposite above: While engaged in shelling enemy positions on 13 May, the monitor M30 was sunk by Turkish shore batteries along the Gulf of Smyrna. The M30 was one of many small coastal monitors hastily ordered in the early part of the war and built to bombard German and Turkish shore instillations.

Opposite below: Shells are here being loaded onto Admiral Beatty's flagship *Lion* at the beginning of 1916. Nobody could have predicted the disaster that would soon arise from the way those shells and the charges that fired them were stored.

The Battle of Jutland, 31 May 1916

The Grand Fleet leaves port, ready to take on the might of the German navy. In 1916 the Royal Navy still possessed the most powerful seaborne force in the world.

Preparing for the clash of the giants – the 1st Battlecruiser Squadron heads out to sea prior to the Battle of Jutland.

The Grand Fleet at sea, led by Admiral Jellicoe in the battleship *Iron Duke* – in Churchill's words, Jellicoe was 'the only man who could have lost the war in a single afternoon'. It was a responsibility that weighed heavily on the admiral's mind.

First, Second, Third, Fourth Light-Cruiser Squadrons.
4th, 11th, 12th, Destroyer Flotillas

The German High Sea Fleet Running for Port.

Derfflinger.   Rood.   Fortune.   Tipperary   Hindenberg.   Kaiserin.   Oestfriesland.   Rostock.
Four German Destroyers Sinking.   Onslaught.

The Torpedo Attack (at night) by the British Light Cruisers and Destroyers against the German High Sea Fleet,
at the Great Battle of Jutland, May 31st–June 1st, 1916. The British lost 14 ships and the Germans 21.
Passed by Admiralty for Publication

ABRAHAMS & SONS,
DEVONPORT.   698

The battle began just before 4 p.m., when the two battlecruiser fleets sighted each other off Jutland. Playing his part perfectly, Admiral Hipper immediately turned and fled; Beatty, his blood up, followed him, little realising that Admiral Scheer and the entire High Seas Fleet were waiting just over the horizon.

Opposite above: The Battle of Jutland, the greatest naval encounter of the war, took place on the afternoon of 31 May 1916. The end result was stalemate although the British retained control of the North Sea and could justifiably claim victory. This artist-drawn view of the action is atmospheric but totally inaccurate. Most of the ships fought at a distance of many miles.

Opposite below: The German plan to lure Admiral Beatty with his fleet of battlecruisers and, if possible, part of Jellicoe's more ponderous battle fleet under the guns of the High Seas Fleet almost worked – thanks to the impetuosity of Beatty.

Admiral Hipper is shown here on the deck on his flagship *Seydlitz*, flanked by members of his staff. An astute and capable commander, Hipper knew he had to stay clear of the British battlecruisers but that did not stop his ships keeping up an accurate and, as it turned out, deadly rate of fire on the pursuing enemy. The German gunnery was astonishingly accurate, taking Beatty and all of the British sailors by surprise.

Within minutes of the first shots being fired, both the *Lion* and *Tiger* were straddled and then hit. The *Lion* was lucky not to sink when a cordite flash nearly exploded her magazine. More significantly, early in the action the *Indefatigable* received a direct hit and, thanks to the standard procedure on Beatty's battlecruisers of leaving open the anti-flash doors to the magazine, exploded in a ball of flame. Only two men survived the terrible explosion.

Further disaster came within minutes. The *Queen Mary*, like the *Indefatigable*, blew up after being hit by shells from the German ships. Only eleven men out of a crew of 1,275 managed to survive the explosion.

A German photograph showing the end of the battlecruiser *Queen Mary*. The successful destruction of the two British battlecruisers in the opening moments of the battle astounded both the Germans and the British.

ADMIRAL. LORD CHATFIELD

Ernie Chatfield, later Admiral of the Fleet but Beatty's flag captain on the *Lion* at Jutland, was the recipient of his admiral's now famous remark after the second battlecruiser blew up: 'There seems to be something wrong with our bloody ships today, Chatfield.' Tragically, Beatty never accepted or even understood that by condoning the practices of leaving magazine doors open and stacking unwrapped cordite charges on the deck, he had contributed to the deaths of so many men.

Admiral Beatty's flagship *Lion*, blazing furiously, after taking several hits in the early stages of the battle. The *Tiger* and the *Princess Royal* were also damaged. The commander of *Princess Royal* ran against the popular practice in the battlecruiser fleet and had the magazine doors on his ship firmly closed – it saved lives and his ship!

Despite the loss of two ships, the British battlecruisers continued to fight and, gradually, they began to achieve some success. Hipper's flagship, the *Seydlitz*, was set on fire and forced to limp out of the action.

The *Derfflinger*, shown here firing a broadside, also received considerable punishment during the battlecruiser encounter.

The damage to the *Derfflinger* can be seen in this German photograph, taken once Hipper's battlecruiser force had limped back to port.

Damage to the *Derfflinger* is seen here – from inside the battered hull.

The battlecruiser *Lützow*, launched only in 1915, was another victim of the action. Severely damaged by British broadsides, during the night she gradually settled lower and lower in the water. It was clear that she could not make it back to base and was, consequently, sunk by her own forces rather than allowed to fall into British hands.

Admiral Scheer

Admiral Reinhard Scheer, mastermind of the German plan and commander-in-chief of the High Seas Fleet. Like Jellicoe, Scheer was mindful of his responsibilities but had, perhaps, a more imaginative outlook on the war and his part in it.

Even as Beatty turned away, leaving Admiral Sir Hugh Evan Thomas and his squadron of four battleships to cover his withdrawal, the British suffered another catastrophic loss. The *Invincible* – yet another victim of open magazine doors – exploded in a ball of flame.

Admiral Horace Hood, commander of the 3rd Battlecruiser Squadron, who died along with over a thousand of his men when the *Invincible* exploded. He was one of two British admirals to die at Jutland.

The *Von der Tann*, another of Hipper's battlecruisers severely damaged in the running fight between the two fleets.

Admiral Beatty – hero or villain of Jutland, depending on your stance.

England Expects—

and

England must not—and will not be disappointed.

RECRUITS WANTED
FOR THE
ROYAL NAVAL DIVISION
To serve during the Period of the War

AGE 18 TO 38 - MEAN CHEST MEASUREMENT 34 inches
HEIGHT 5 ft. 3½ inches.

There are NO EXPENSES incurred in joining
FREE KITS and FOOD being provided.

Men are paid at the Service Rate of 1/3 per day - Separation
allowances are made to the families of Married Men.

Apply to :-
THE ROYAL NAVAL DIVISION.
Recruiting Office : 112 THE STRAND, LONDON. W.C.

'England Expects', a recruiting poster unashamedly playing on the myth and glory of Nelson.

WHO made these little Islands the centre of the greatest and most powerful Empire the world has ever seen? *Our Forefathers*

WHO ruled this Empire with such wisdom and sympathy that every part of it–of whatever race or origin–has rallied to it in its hour of need? *Our Fathers*

WHO will stand up to preserve this great and glorious heritage? *We will*

WHO will remember us with pride and exultation and thankfulness if we do our duty to-day? *Our Children*

JUSTIFY THE FAITH OF YOUR FATHERS, AND EARN THE GRATITUDE OF YOUR ———CHILDREN———

ENLIST TO-DAY!

Published by THE PARLIAMENTARY RECRUITING COMMITTEE, LONDON.—Poster No. 96.   T126 Wt W 423-406. 10,000. 4/15. Gd J. C. & S.

Enlist Today – the glorious history of Britain is here used to get men to enlist.

A US Navy recruiting poster from early 1916.

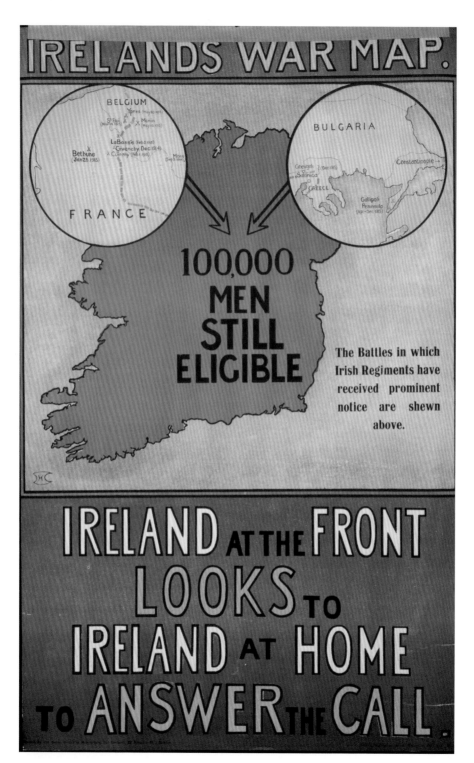

Ireland's war map – thousands of Irish soldiers and sailors joined the armed forces between 1914 and 1918.

'Here is Opportunity', reads the poster, join up and see the world.

A poster for the London Patriotic Recruiting meetings.

John Bull is depicted here, defying enemy ships and Zeppelins.

A poster advertising the 1916 flag day for the RNLI.

Come On You Sea-Cooks

The big German liners which the Government is now fitting out as Army transports need a large Commissary Staff, and the Navy wants American citizens and aliens of friendly nations with first papers to serve as Cooks, Stewards and Mess Attendants on board these ships going abroad; men who are to cook and prepare the food and serve it. Here is a first-class job and working for the Navy makes you a better man. Your pay begins at once; you are never laid off because of bad business or hard times and if you are sick you get your money just the same. In the Navy you associate with clean, high-minded men under healthy conditions with plenty of things to eat and with a lot of sports and amusements. Remember, everything is free, board and lodging, and so is your first outfit of clothing. By joining the Messmen Branch of the American Navy, you are not only helping your Country but also yourself.

THIS IS WHAT YOU CAN EARN

Chief Commissary Steward	$83.00	Cabin Cook	$55.50
Commissary Steward	72.00	Wardroom Steward	61.00
Ship's Cook 1st class	66.00	Wardroom Cook	55.50
Ship's Cook 2nd class	52.00	Steerage Steward	46.50
Ship's Cook 3rd class	41.00	Steerage Cook	41.00
Ship's Cook 4th class	35.50	Warrant Officers' Steward	46.50
Baker 1st class	55.50	Warrant Officers' Cook	41.00
Baker 2nd class	46.50	Mess Attendant 1st class	41.00
Cabin Steward	61.00	Mess Attendant 2nd class	35.50
	Mess Attendant 3rd class	$37.00	

Enlist in Naval Reserve Force - For the War Only

Apply to Nearest Navy Recruiting Station

'Come on you Sea-Cooks' – the US Navy seeks recruits of a specialist nature.

British Armed Sea-plane on Patrol. R.N.A.S.

PASSED FOR PUBLICATION
BY PRESS BUREAU, 27 OCT. 1917.

From the beginning of the war the Royal Naval Air Service took responsibility for the defence of Britain's coast, using seaplanes and blimps to mount regular patrols.

OUT FOR VICTORY.

THE DESTROYER CAPTAIN.
Blow high, blow low, he's there!

A patriotic postcard from 1916, showing one of the new, glamorous heroes of the war
– the destroyer captain.

Sailors from a US warship carrying out drill.

A fishing fleet heading for the British coast, bringing much-needed provisions and supplies.

ROYAL NAVY
Nº 21.

TAKING STORES
TO WARSHIPS

Storing a warship, always a tiring but crucially important task.

A humorous postcard, reminding the general public that Britain's Navy was always ready and always willing to fight the enemy.

As the scale of the war and the need for manpower expanded, women were recruited to take over administrative and other shore-based roles.

'The Watchers of the Seas.' The Royal Navy continued its blockade of Germany despite the sortie by the High Seas Fleet that led to the Battle of Jutland.

With Beatty having reversed the situation, now leading the German ships into a trap similar to the one that Scheer had devised, the main fleets came into contact at 6.30 at night, just as light was beginning to fail. Sporadic contact and firing were maintained until 8.30. This photograph shows the battleships *Warspite* and *Malaya* during this stage of the battle.

The *Friedrich der Grosse*, flagship of Admiral Scheer during the Battle of Jutland. Launched and completed in 1912, she was armed with ten 12-inch guns.

Opposite above: The action during the hours of early darkness on 31 May was confused and complicated as both sides strove hard to gain the advantage. The German battleship *Pommern* had already been hit by shells from Beatty's battlecruisers when she was caught and torpedoed by the destroyer *Onslaught*. The old battleship immediately broke in two and sank. There were no survivors.

Opposite below: The battlecruiser *Tiger* was hit by over twenty shells during the battle – she was repaired in less than a month.

13200 t Wasserverdrängung.
18-18,6 sm Schnelligkeit.
16000 Pferdest.
21,5 m Länge
22,2 m Breite.
7,7 m Tiefgang.
729 Mann Besatzung.

Linienschiff S.M.S. "Pommern."

H.M.S. TIGER

A broadside from HMS *Warspite*, her eight 15-inch guns creating huge amounts of smoke – making life more than a little difficult for spotters and rangefinders. The Admiralty had consistently refused to use a computerised firing system, similar to the one used by the Germans, invented by Arthur Pollen and known as the Argo Clock system, before war even began. It was a failure that had dire results for British gunnery.

Admiral John Jellicoe is shown here on the deck of his flagship. Jellicoe knew that he had a golden chance to destroy Scheer and the whole of the German Fleet. He also knew that there could well be U-boats in the vicinity. He would do nothing to endanger the Grand Fleet and in the early hours of 1 June he called off the pursuit, something that later caused him to be accused of overcautiousness during the battle.

In the end it was all in vain as Scheer managed to slip past the cruisers and destroyers that constituted the rearguard of the British Fleet and make it back to Germany. A number of skirmishes between these light vessels and German forces took place as Scheer and Hipper tried desperately to break through the British fleet. Ships on both sides were lost. This photograph shows the damage sustained by the light cruiser *Chester* in the action.

The legend of Boy (First Class) John Travers Cornwell, a sixteen-year-old gun layer on the *Chester*, has gone down in history. With the rest of his gun crew dead and Cornwell himself mortally wounded, the boy stuck to his post until the end. By his courage and devotion to duty, Cornwell earned himself a Victoria Cross, awarded posthumously after he died in hospital at Harwich a day or so later.

The armoured cruiser *Defence* was the flagship of Rear Admiral Sir Robert Arbuthnot, commander of the 1st Cruiser Squadron. Shortly after 6.00 p.m., the squadron was chasing a group of German scouts when out of the dusk loomed the huge bulk of Admiral Hipper's battlecruiser force. Almost immediately, the *Defence* was hit by two salvoes. A huge black cloud engulfed the ship. When it had cleared *Defence* had vanished.

Admiral Arbuthnot, who died when his ship *Defence* exploded under accurate fire from the enemy battlecruisers, at approximately 6.15 p.m. on 31 May. Nearly 900 sailors died with him – there were no survivors.

The cruiser *Warrior* was also part of Arbuthnot's squadron and was hit several times before she could pull away. She lost steam from her engines and lay, a sitting duck, in the path of the enemy. The lucky intervention of the battleship *Warspite* – actually out of control and heading straight for Hipper's battlecruisers – saved her but clearly the *Warrior* was critically damaged. She was taken in tow by the seaplane carrier *Engadine* but, during the night, the weather deteriorated and *Warrior* finally sank below the waves.

The seaplane carrier *Engadine*, which attempted to tow the stricken *Warrior* back to port – the huge hangar on her rear deck can be clearly seen. The *Engadine* had already taken part in air raids on Germany and, during the Battle of Jutland, became the first ship to fly off a heavier-than-air machine during a naval battle. The aircraft provided information for Jellicoe and his staff.

H M S "BLACK PRINCE" IN ROUGH SEA

The *Black Prince*, another of Arbuthnot's unlucky cruisers, is shown here in heavy seas. She received many hits from the German battlecruisers before she, too, was sunk. The fourth ship in the squadron, the *Duke of Edinburgh*, managed to escape.

At dawn on 1 June Admiral Jellicoe found his fleet spread out across the North Sea. But of the German High Seas Fleet, there was no sign. He had won the day and, with the threat of submarine attack growing more likely by the hour, he ordered a return to Scapa Flow and Rosyth.

The High Seas Fleet had lost fewer ships (eleven German compared to fourteen British) and with 2,545 men killed, compared to 6,097 British, they claimed a victory. However, their ships had sustained considerably more damage and several of them never sailed again. This shows the damage to Hipper's flagship *Seydlitz*.

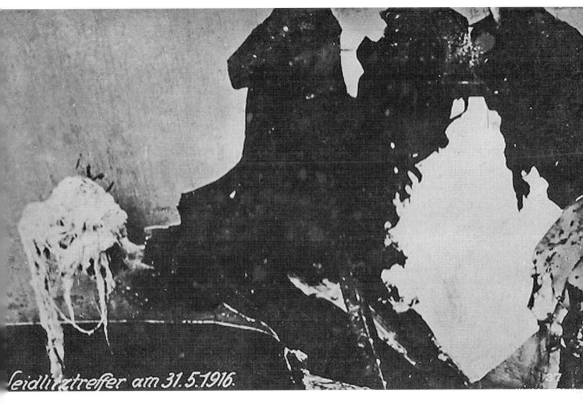

A close-up view of shell damage to the hull of the *Seydlitz* gives a good indication of the power of naval projectiles at this time.

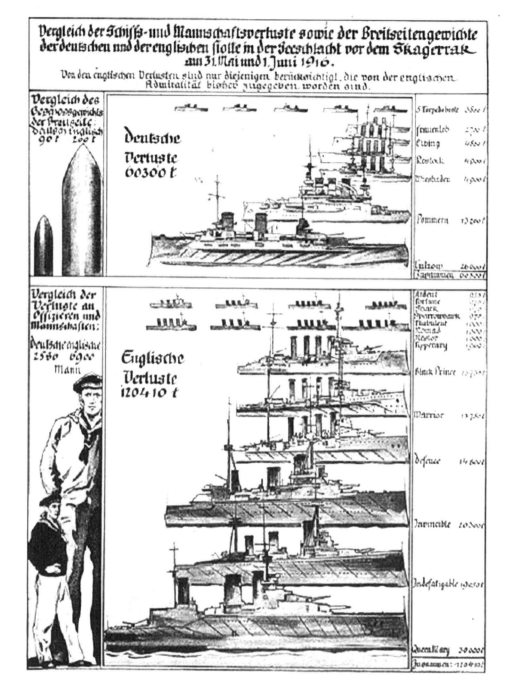

Keen to get every last ounce of prestige from the battle, the German press machine was soon in full flow. This postcard from 1916 trumpets the respective losses of Germany and Britain. As someone once said, the battle was a tactical victory for Germany but a strategic one for Britain as the High Seas Fleet never sailed again – apart from one brief sortie in August 1916 when Scheer put to sea but immediately turned back once he learned that the Grand Fleet was lurking nearby.

It wasn't just the High Seas Fleet that was mauled at the battle; British ships also suffered at the hands of the more accurate German shellfire. This shows damage to the battleship *Barham*.

More damage to the *Barham*.

The grave and memorial stone of some of the men killed on the *Barham* during the battle.

The battleship *Warspite* took several heavy hits in the battle and, for a while at least, with her steering gear out of action, she careered across the ocean, totally out of control. This photograph shows just some of the damage she sustained.

The battlecruiser *Tiger*, seriously damaged during the Battle of Jutland, is shown here in dry dock for repairs.

A commemorative postcard showing the battleship *Ajax*, a relatively modern addition to the Fleet, which survived the encounter with few casualties. She went on, after Jutland, to serve in the Mediterranean, and was finally scrapped in 1926.

The *Von der Tann* survived Jutland but played no further part in the war. She was later surrendered with the rest of the High Seas Fleet in 1918.

Arguably, with ships like the mighty *Iron Duke* at his command, Jellicoe could have done better at the Battle of Jutland. He had a numerically superior force at his disposal and at nightfall on 31 May was in a position to decimate Scheer and the whole German fleet. He was the subject of much criticism after the battle, most of it declaring that he had been too cautious.

M.S. IRON DUKE, ADMIRAL JELLICOE'S FLAGSHIP (READY FOR ACTI

Jellicoe kept tight-lipped about his part in the action but defended the conduct of David Beatty, a man who really could have lost the war in a few short hours. By squashing the report that criticised the procedure on the battlecruisers of leaving magazine doors open and unwrapping and stacking cordite shells in passageways or on the deck, Jellicoe undoubtedly saved Beatty's career. By November Jellicoe had been 'shoved upstairs' to become First Sea Lord while David Beatty took over as Commander-in-Chief of the Grand Fleet.

Whoever won the Battle of Jutland, Britain certainly did not lose it. The Royal Navy retained control of the sea and, perhaps more importantly, those in command in Berlin realised it. From June 1916 onwards, the main effort of the German navy was directed towards the U-boat war, a much surer way, their planners thought, of bringing Britain to her knees.

A British broadside, clearly showing the power of the Royal Navy. That power continued to haunt Germany long after the Battle of Jutland was consigned to the history books.

June

Field Marshal Kitchener is seen here leaving the *Iron Duke* while on a visit to the fleet. Kitchener's importance had declined considerably since the heady days of 1914, when his face seemed to be leering from every hording, wall or fence. Yet he was still highly regarded by the public, and by Britain's allies. The Tsar of Russia in particular felt that a visit from the famous man would help boost Russian resolve. As a consequence, in early June Kitchener boarded the cruiser *Hampshire* and set off for Russia.

On 5 June the *Hampshire* struck a mine off the Orkney Islands – a mine originally laid to catch the Grand Fleet as it left port – and quickly sank in heavy seas. Due to the terrible weather, it was not possible to launch any boats and the cruiser sank in just ten minutes. Kitchener, clearly knowing his fate, was last seen walking calmly on the quarterdeck, talking to the crew. There were just twelve survivors. Kitchener was not among them.

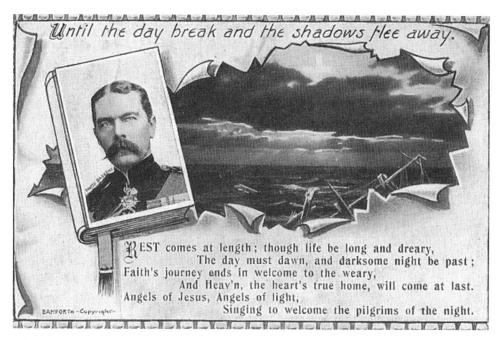

Kitchener's body was never recovered and this led to a belief, in some quarters, that he was not dead but engaged in a secret mission. He would soon return, it was said, with a secret formula for winning the war. It was not to be. Kitchener was dead, his time over. This memorial card was quickly printed and sold in its thousands to devastated members of the British public.

On 18 June the destroyer *Eden* was sunk in the English Channel after a collision with the transport she was escorting, the SS *France*. Captain Farquhar and forty-two men were drowned; another thirty-three were rescued by the transport.

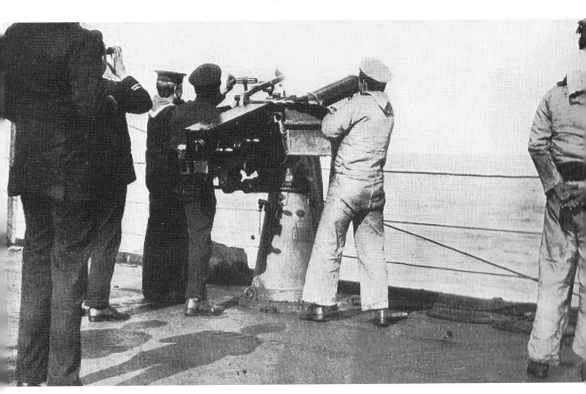

Bombardment of enemy positions along the French and Belgian coasts continued throughout the war. This shows one of the quick-firing guns on a British monitor of the Dover Patrol, in action in the Channel.

The monitor HMS *Severn*, one of several big-gun ships used to bombard the enemy coast.

King George
inspects Bluejackets
on Iron Duke.

Royal visits to ships of the Grand Fleet happened regularly throughout
the war. This shows King George on board the *Iron Duke*, flagship of
the Fleet.

July

British cruisers lay down a smokescreen, one of many new tactics brought in during the war, more than useful for the protection of capital ships.

No 13.

Le S S. Brussels renfloué et son héroïque capitaine Fryatt.
The S S. "Brussels" set afloat again and her heroic Captain Fryatt.
Het stoomschip Brussels vlot gebracht. Zijn heldhaftigen kapitein Fryatt.

Captain Charles Algernon Fryatt was the master of a number of different cross-Channel passenger ships during the war years. In compliance with the advice of Winston Churchill (who insisted that U-boat crews were felons and should be dealt with accordingly), he had, on at least three occasions, tried to ram U-boats – once, when in command of the SS *Wrexham*, a U-boat had chased him for 40 miles. On 25 June he took his ship *Brussels* out of the Hook of Holland, bound for Harwich. The *Brussels* was soon surrounded by five German destroyers and Fryatt and his crew taken ashore, where they were interned. The legend, probably apocryphal, says that German agents on board the *Brussels* showed lights to guide the destroyers to their target.

Fryatt was put on trial, charged with sinking the U33, even though the U-boat had not been destroyed. Fryatt had, indeed, attempted to ram the submarine in March of that year but she had crash-dived and escaped. Fryatt was found guilty and, although he was a civilian, sentenced to death. At 1900 hours on 21 July he was shot by firing squad. The execution was condemned by the British as 'sheer murder' but the Germans insisted that Fryatt had gone beyond trying to defend his ship and taken offensive action.

No 12.   Le S. S. Brussels coulé à l'extrémité du Môle et son héroïque capitaine Fryatt, capturé par les Boches le 23 juin 1916 et fusillé le 27 juillet 1916.
The S. S. " Brussels " sunk near the extremity of Zeebrugge-Môle, and her heroic Captain Fryatt, who was captured by the germans on the 23rd June 1916 and shot on the 27th July 1916.

When Fryatt was interned his ship, the *Brussels*, was taken into Zeebrugge and then Brest, where she spent the rest of the war. In the wake of the Allied advance in the autumn of 1918 she was scuttled by the Germans.

After Jutland the growing U-boat fleet, always a significant weapon, became the main German focus. One of the small U-boats employed around the German coast is shown here about to leave the safety of Dunkirk.

Attacking from the surface remained the preference for most U-boat commanders. This drawing shows a U-boat shelling a merchant ship that is travelling alone and unguarded across the Atlantic. As losses mounted, the call for a convoy system grew more vocal but, in 1916, the Admiralty was clear – convoys would be unworkable as they did not believe merchant ship captains had the skills to muster and maintain formation. Providing suitable escorts was also a problem.

The trawling fleets of Britain continued to operate throughout the war, despite the fact that many of them had been requisitioned by the Admiralty for use as minesweepers. Inshore boats, like the ones shown here, became increasingly important.

August

The quarterdeck of HMS *Dreadnought* – the photograph gives a good idea of the open and vulnerable conditions in which sailors had to work.

Group of Submarines in Torquay Harbour.

On 9 August the submarine B10 was bombed and sunk by Austrian aircraft while undergoing repair in Venice, the first British submarine to be sunk by an aeroplane. This view shows the submarine alongside her sister ships B6 and B11 in Torquay harbour.

The German submarine U38 successfully attacked and sank the Q-ship *Remembrance* in the Aegean on 14 August. Q-ships, sometimes known as Mystery Ships, were heavily armed merchant vessels with their guns disguised and looking for all the world like down-at-heel tramp steamers, not worth wasting a torpedo on. Their aim was to lure enemy submarines to the surface, where the Q-ship's guns would, hopefully, take care of the U-boat. Sometimes, however, the deception ended in disaster with a sudden torpedo – as with the U38 and the *Remembrance*.

The Q-ship *Privet*. With the number of sinkings to submarines mounting by the week, the advent of Q-ships like the *Privet* was, for a while at least, a successful if rather dangerous way of countering the menace.

The boxes shown here hide one of the 4-inch guns on the Q-ship *Hyderabad*. Viewed through a periscope, the covered guns would look like an ordinary deck cargo.

Sailors gather around the bomb throwers on the deck of the 'mystery ship' *Hyderabad* – bomb throwers were useful weapons should the U-boat try to submerge.

An artist's impression of a submarine passing a destroyer, her deck awash and only the conning tower really breaking the surface. Low in the water and sleek, the submarines were difficult to spot from the deck of a merchantman or warship.

On 15 August 1916 the *Furious* was launched from the yards of Armstrong Whitworth on the Tyne. Originally designed and laid down as a battlecruiser, the *Furious* was converted into an aircraft carrier, with the flight deck forward and an 18-inch gun aft. This view shows her after her full conversion into a carrier.

Opposite above: On 19 August the German battleship *Westfalen* was torpedoed by E23 in the Gulf of Riga. The *Westfalen* managed to limp back to port where, contrary to some reports, she was soon repaired.

Opposite below: On 19 August, the same day that *Westfalen* was torpedoed by a British submarine, the light cruiser *Nottingham* was sunk after she was hit by three torpedoes from the U52. The *Nottingham* was engaged in a sweep of the North Sea and a dense fog shielded the approach of the submarine. The U-boat assisted in the rescue of *Nottingham*'s crew and very few lives were lost.

Deutschlands Dreadnoughts

S. M. S. „Westfalen"

Erbaut: Weser-Werft Bremen.

Länge	146 Meter	Deplacement ca.	19,000 Tonnen
Größte Breite	27,00 „	Maschinenleistung ca.	20,000 P.S
Tiefgang ca.	8,10 „	Geschwindigkeit	19 Knoten

The British submarine E9 with its commander, the famous Max Horton, inset.

September

The battleship *Emperor of India*, sister ship to the *Iron Duke*, is shown here in the Grand Harbour at Malta. After missing the Battle of Jutland, she served primarily in the Mediterranean and, later, in the Atlantic. She was eventually used as a target ship before being sold for scrap in 1931.

S.S. "NESTOR." SYDNEY.
UROPEAN WAR. 1914-1919.

The Blue Funnel Line ship *Nestor* served mainly in the seas around Australia. She was used primarily as a troop carrier during the war years.

At the Pier, Pembroke Dock.

The County Class cruiser *Essex* is shown here during her fitting out at Hobbs Point in Pembroke Dockyard.

Admiral William Reginald 'Blinker' Hall, Director of Naval Intelligence from 1914 until 1919, was known as 'Blinker' – though not to his face – because of a slight facial tic. He was the man responsible for the creation and running of Room 40, the codebreaking centre, at the Admiralty – the forerunner of Bletchley Park.

Experiments with aircraft taking off from runways on board ship – usually over the forward guns – continued right through the war.

October

Battleships patrolling in a heavy sea.

With the blockade of Germany having to be maintained at all times, coaling at sea was sometimes necessary. Sailors hated the whole process of taking on coal – doing it while at sea was even more unpleasant.

On the night of 26/27 October, a flotilla of German destroyers and torpedo boats managed to slip through the barrage at the mouth of the Channel and attack shipping in the Dover area. This shows a group of German torpedo boats moored up after the raid. The destroyer *Flirt* was torpedoed in the raid.

The destroyer *Nubian* was also torpedoed in the raid of 27 October, when she was chasing the retreating German ships. Her bows were blown off and the ship beached at South Foreland. This shows part of the wreck. The aft section of the *Nubian* was later joined with the bows of another damaged destroyer, the *Zulu*, to make a ship known as the *Zubian*.

November

With the High Seas Fleet confined to port, surface action for the German navy increasingly depended on small vessels such as destroyers and torpedo boats. It meant that, on the British side, the ships of the Dover Patrol became vitally important. This photograph shows the Tribal Class destroyer HMS *Crusader* passing the mole at Dover.

The famous HMS *Broke* of the Dover Patrol.

Submarine B11 passing a line of moored battleships.

The *Britannic* was the third and largest in the Olympic class of liners that included the *Titanic* in their number. Launched just before the war, she was converted into a hospital ship in 1915. On 21 November, off Kea in the Greek islands, the ship was rocked by an underwater explosion, probably as a result of hitting a mine, and sank in just fifty-five minutes.

This shows the launch of the *Britannic* from the same Belfast yards that had produced the *Titanic*. Only thirty people died when she struck the mine, the rest of the 1,066 people on board quickly taking to the lifeboats. She was the largest ship lost during the First World War.

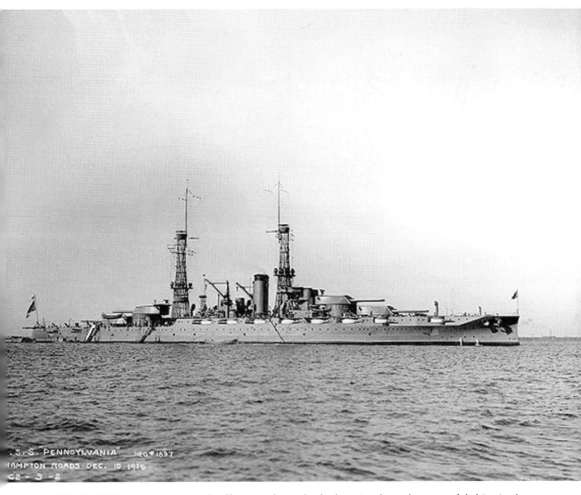

With the USA remaining neutral, officers and men looked enviously at the powerful ships in the American navy. This shows the USS *Pennsylvania*, a ship that would have been invaluable in a battle like Jutland.

Another view of the strength of the US naval forces; this photograph is a close-up view of the gun turrets of an American Dreadnought.

December

The cruiser *Fearless* on patrol in the North Sea.

By courtesy of]   [Smith's Dock Company.

FROM WAR TO PEACE.

The former Monitor 34 converted into the Oil-Tanker " Satoe "
(Anglo-Saxon Petroleum Co., Ltd.).

Despite the caption, this photograph shows the monitor No. 24 – there was no monitor numbered 34 as the caption declares. She is seen here in post-war years, when she was converted into an oil tanker.

Neutral ships, like this one from Denmark, often painted their nationality on the sides of their hulls. It rarely stopped the Royal Navy from investigating the vessels concerned.

On 4 December the destroyer *Llewellyn* sank the U36 off Dover. It was the first successful use of depth charges in the war.

Ein Torpedoboot als Depeschenboot der Flotte.

This shows German torpedo boats in heavy seas – life on board these tiny vessels must have been wet and uncomfortable.

Torpedobootsdurchbruch in der Skagerakschlacht. (Originalaufnahme)

154

German torpedo boats operating in the Skagerrak – the torpedo tubes are clearly identifiable on the deck of the lead vessel.

Despite the war, ships still had to be built – if nothing else, then to replace those vessels lost in the conflict. This shows the launch of a light cruiser from the Welsh yard at Pembroke Dock.

British submarines lie moored against the side of their tender, HMS *Hazard*. Originally built as a cruiser, the *Hazard* was later lost in a collision in the English Channel.

A little rest and recuperation – sailors on the beach!

Shay Alf, old man, you're gone quite bald!— you're worrying too mush about thish war, y'know!

Right: Humour could be guaranteed to see the British through most trials and tribulations. The overuse of alcohol was, however, frowned upon, and licensing laws were introduced to stop people imbibing too much and too frequently.

Below: The cost of waging the war could never be forgotten, no matter how much people were able to laugh away their problems. This shows a wounded sailor being winched on board a hospital ship.

When all was said and done, the British public could always content itself with the thought that the Royal Navy was there to protect their shores. This shows the powerful battleship *Erin*, originally built for the Turkish navy as the *Reshadieh* and commandeered at the outbreak of war.

The 12-inch gun battleship *Superb* is shown here leaving Elswick, a symbol of everything that was strong and right with the Royal Navy.